Dear Son,

One day,
You will find yourself on a bike,
Speeding

     down

         a

             hill,

Traveling faster than your feet can peddle,
Ahead of you, you will see a busy intersection,
Like so many Prostell's before you,

you will remain calm,
Knowing the 2-3 seconds between You & certain Death

is more than enough time to apply your brakes,

You will apply your brakes,
Nothing will happen,
Know that in THAT moment,
You are alive,

One day,
You will meet a girl,
Her hair will smell like honey dew,
Her smile will freeze you in your tracks,

Everytime,

You will hand her your heart,
In a neatly pressed, perfumed envelope,
Which she will immediately open and blush,
She will momentarily bask in the warm energy that is your love,
And then she will put that envelope down on her dresser and forget it

1

ever existed,
She is doing you a favor,

Son,
Know that from the moment you were born,
There were people whose very lives where dedicated to seeing your destruction,
Also note,
The many more who fought, bled, even died in order to guarantee your success,
Understand that you are equally indebted to both for the remarkable resilience that you will develop,

Know that there are those who will hate you because you do not look like them,
And also those that will hate you because you do,
This is exactly as confusing and messed up as it sounds,
Do not waste a moment on it,

One day,
You will stand face to face with your fears,
You will look them square in the eye,
And you will turn and run away,
Do not be ashamed,
You will meet them again,
This time you will be Bigger,
You will be Stronger,
You will be Wiser,
You will now be Qualified,

To hold the hand of those who have not yet learned that courage is not the opposite of fear,
Just the willingness to move forward despite it,

Son,
You come from a line of articulate Men,
Know it has not always been this way,
Before there were love poems,
There were angry letters and phone calls,

Before that doors slamming, and backs turned,
Before that welts seared onto backsides, arms and legs,
Before that revolvers lowered from foreheads and holstered,
Bottles, pills, and powder put down never to be picked up again,
60+ hour work weeks for decades that left bodies and minds bent over and broken,
Know that they all said the same thing, Son, I Love You.

One Day,
You will come to me,
I will tell you, Son you are wrong,
Do not do that,
Choose another option, Son
And You,
You will turn around, You will walk out of that door,
You will do EXACTLY what I asked you NOT to do,
Because of this,
You will experience pain,
Heartache,
Turmoil,
And I will NEVER be more proud of you,
You owe your beautiful face to your Mother,
You owe your hard head to your Father,
Everything else is yours,
You owe no justification nor explanation to ANYONE for the man you are,

Son, one day,
You may meet a boy,
Don't be alarmed, he will be naked,
He will be so small, yet he will be the biggest thing you have ever seen,
His hands will be so tiny,
Yet he will steal your heart from your chest,
Little Thief,
He will take your very breath,
This is OK,
Immediately you will know you would give him your last,
Pay Attention Son,
He is here to teach you,

3

Things that I never could, that no one else can, listen to him,
He will show you so much,
About life,
About love,
About a Power that lies in you that YOU never imagined,
In exchange,
All he will ask,
is to know you,

Sounds crazy I know,
But trust me, it will be the greatest thing you will ever do.

Pardon my self-indulgence.

I know.

This is not the way books are supposed to open up but let me address that this way; So?

This is my book.

My second book, my first poetic effort so, eh.

I believe that's how you spell that. If not, eh.

Even more important than this being my book, I felt very strongly about the need to open up this book with that particular piece. No Table of contents. No preface. Just words Dear Son.

The truth is I hope to sell a million copies of this effort.

By Sunday.

On the outside chance that doesn't happen, then the message is reason enough for to consider this volume a success. Shortly after I completed my memoir "The Perks Cult Life or why I had to slap brother Ronnie 7 times", I was riding in the car with my son who was 7 years old at the time. As we drove along I looked over and he is reading the section where I tell about us being reunited after forces within the UNOI (the cult) conspired to keep us apart. He couldn't have been more than 4 when this happened so I asked him if he remembered that day. He tells me yes he does and starts telling me what he was thinking at the time. If I never sold another book, that conversation alone made it well worth writing and publishing.

And so it is with this collection of poetry. I began writing and performing poetry in 2010 in the midst of leaving the UNOI. I found it an amazing opportunity to share the truth and light that been gifted to me as well as an invaluable means of self-expression.

As I began to delve deeper and deeper into poetry it only made sense to me that I would have no shortage of pieces about the most important relationships in my life; my relationship with my children. And sure enough nothing came.

There were poems about love, revolution, slavery, life, death, music, hip hop, Detroit, the UNOI, traffic, relationships, and sex (not necessarily in that order of appearance). Alas, no matter how long I sat and meditated, no matter how close or far we were, no words ever came to aptly describe our relationship.

During that time I grew closer and closer to my own Father, Prostell Jr. and that closeness gave me a deeper and more profound understanding of our place in the diaspora of African American fatherhood but still nothing came.

Never one to force things I was contented to keep waiting and keep writing until the right words arrived.

Then one day I was in Denver, riding my bike on the way to the Freedom of Speech poetry series hosted by the powerful woman known as Lady Speech. As one often does when riding a bicycle in Denver I found myself zooming down a hill at about a 60 degree angle.

To understand what happened next one may need a mild background in mechanical engineering. The way modern American bikes are designed, when you press the brake they are supposed to either slow down or stop. Got that? In this case that didn't happen and I found myself hurtling toward Colorado Avenue (for those who have never been to Denver, Colorado Avenue is busy right now. No I don't care what time you are reading this. It is ALWAYS a bad time to have no brakes heading downhill onto this street.)

I am writing this now so I am fairly certain I did not die that day, although I do not know how. What I do know is that the words that open this book came to me and instantly I knew they were the ones I had been waiting on. Sort of like my Sons.

As I began to share these words with friends and family, I saw that these sentiments are not unique to me and that a Father's love for his Son is something that transcends race, religion, demographic, economics, and yes even gender. I share them now in hopes that they

6

mean something to you, but knowing that one day my son will pick up this book when I am not around and perhaps understand what I waited so long to find the words to say. I Love You, Son.

Also included in this volume are a cross section of poetry some of which includes a brief (I hope) description of where these words and idea come from. I thank you for taking the time experience them.

Peace and Light

Prostell

Kandi

You're probably expecting something like......
He raised his automatic weapon like the hand of God,
Squeezing then releasing a flurry of bullets,
That ripped through the midnight air like a meteor shower,
Cutting through space and time,
Tearing the atmosphere,
Smashing into the earth that was this little girl's mind,
Ripping flesh from Bone,
Splintering bone into brain matter,
Eradicating the very essence of her, instantly,
Thoughts...memories...dreams...hopes of other that resided in her,
evaporating into nothing,
'

'

But in reality,
All you get is a phone call,
The all too familiar sound of a teenage girl crying into the other end of
the line,
Kandi is dead,
Shot in the back of the head,
Fleeing the crack house where she had stashed herself,
1 too many nights trying to escape an adverse home life,

If there were any justice to be found in Poetry,
Then she would be standing on this stage,
And I would be somewhere out there,
bragging to you how I used to know her,
Instead I am on this stage,
And I have come to tell you,
I used to know her,
A voice as free and as clear as sunlight,
existing in spaces as dark and as cold as death is,

And this is my greatest fear,
That if I make it too beautiful for you,

That you might mistake,
Her story for art,
That you would take apart,
my method,
And miss entirely the madness in it,

These are not persona pieces,
These are pieces of persons in many cases,
They are all that I have left,

Too many,
Poems penned in the spilled blood of peers passed,
so some days I simply pray for writers block,

And while at the time,
I was a Father of a teenage son,
Who wandered regularly in unfamiliar Central Florida neighborhoods,
I never penned a George Zimmerman piece,
Because when it comes to Trayvon Martins,
My cup runneth over,

No shortage of dead soldjas
So all too often I bury them in this mass grave called poetry,
Find young bodies twisted into awkward shapes on the pavement,
And prop them up as paper swans,
But they are no more decoration
Than the souls hanging from Southern trees are Christmas ornaments,

They are Martyrs,
Involuntary,
Unassuming
I am their disciple,
They live and die in my every breath,
Their heart beats my iambic pentameter,
Their voice echoes in my every word,

CAN YOU HEAR THEIR SCREAM
I did not come to ask you for a 10 or a rewind,
I came to remind you
and mostly myself
of a debt owed that can never be repaid,
of a promise, unfulfilled,
of a beautiful song that I will never,
ever hear

again,

(Another example of a piece I have wanted to write for a very long time and the words just never came. She died back in 1995 this was written in 2013. We were all so young and unfortunately people were dying around us all the time but this was the first one that just took my breath away. Some days I stop and wonder where she'd be today. Smart. Funny. Talented. Streetwise. She was EVEYRTHING. More talent in her pinky than in my body 10X. I put on for Kandi Lee)

Car in Driver

To answer your question

Arthritis has crept into her bones, and conspired with carpal tunnel

T1.3o swell her hands up like balloon animals,

As she painfully grips the wheel,

Trying to muster enough strength and grace to make a simple right hand turn,

Her feet,

Stumble across the peddles like a ballerina who has forgotten her dance steps,

Her mind,

Struggles to adjust to an ever-morphing landscape,

Where shopping plazas spring up, where there were once homes,

Where vacant fields mark burials spots where proud tall building once stood,

And She pauses,

Just for moment because she recognizes,

Something is, , , different,

And YOU,

In the car behind her,

LEAN ON YOUR HORN FOR TEN FULL SECONDS,

Then glare out of your window like a maniac as you screech around her,

Him,

He has some,

Car issues,

A transmission as moody and temperamental as an ex-lover,

That sometimes decides it does NOT want to go into 2nd Gear,

A radiator,

That starts to overheat before he can even make it out of his driveway in the morning,

Yet he somehow manages to keep his cool in bumper to bumper traffic jams,

As he shifts between D and N as though this was a manual transmission

His blinker doesn't work,

So he taps it,

In rhythm with the car in front of him in order to make sure he is in accord with the law,

He must ALWAYS be in accord with the law,

Must wear his seatbelt at all times,

Must always drive 5 miles below the speed limit,

Must never EVER turn on red,

Even if he see no sign that says no turn on red,

His license is 12 months suspended,

And before you ask, the buses no longer run,

From where he can afford to live,

To where they can afford to pay him,

So he makes this his daily pilgrimage, call it a prayer service if you will,

He conducts choir of awkward instruments,

Because the only way they would ever stop him from providing for his family,

Is to take away his car

And/or throw him in jail,

Her,

This is her first time,

Her father sits next to her riding shotgun,

But before he can ever teach her to adjust her mirror or check her blindspot,

You will come along and teach her everything she needs to know about life in the fast lane,

1.Drive defensively

2.The best defense is a good offense,

3. This is no game this is WAR.

4. Speed kills

5. It is better to be the hunter than be the prey

6. America is a melting pot.

7. if you use your horn properly you can say FUCK YOU if 50 different languages

8. It is against the law to drive behind anyone.

9. If they try to get in front of you, SPEED UP!

10. If you get in front them, SLOW DOWN.

11. Don't drive angry.

12. Drive heartless.

And truth is I don't know all of them,

Maybe he is soldier just returned from Iraq and still believes that around every corner,

There is an ied waiting to blow him to smithereens,

Maybe she is a mother with a screaming baby on the back seat,

And another in her womb causing contractions two minutes apart,

Maybe he is just some asshole, , ,

But what I do know is this,

Either these machines we have made,

Have now made us like them,

Cold and inhuman,

Or they have finally revealed us to ourselves

(One day in Orlando my wife went for a walk with our new born baby. She walks back in the door thirty minutes later in tears. Despite the cross walk light, the right of way, and the big baby carriage she was pushing she never made it across the street. I wonder where we are in a rush to. I wonder if you would act like that if we were inside these boxes. I wonder how much time we save driving the way we do. I wonder if those precious seconds are worth the damage we do.)

slave

Are U a slave?

In bondage today,

Because of false promises,

Made to your anscestors,

Or forefathers,

Are U a slave?

Living this lie called the American Dream,

Where Everything's for sale,

Including your self-esteem,

Yet just another cog in this machine,

Just enough chain to peek over the fence,

Just enough gold rope to hang yourself with,

See lap tops and cell phones aint the only thing they've improved on!

Now they got smart Niggas that's so dumb, they think they're free,

Now they got wireless slaves you aint got to chain,

No need for shackles on their ankles when you've locked up their brain,

Give em whipping hands free,

Then call it an application process,

Or call it due process,

Matter fact call it progress,

But I digress,

Are you a slave,

Yes YOU,

Who wished for Blacks to be equal to you,

Hope you really meant cause now your slave too,

Postracial Plantations,

Class warfare,

Where housing bubbles,

And Deregulation are weapons of Mass Destruction,

Do to middle class what Hitler did to the Jew,

Do to everyone else what they do prom dates

Kcuf Em,

Divide and the Conqure,

Black versus White,

Christian versus Muslim,

Gay versus Straight,

Liberal versus Conservatives,

Jacob versus Edward,

Pick a side and there is no middle ground,

Both excess and poverty two stops along the same line,

So I'll ask you,

Are U a slave?

Perhaps an overseer

See and overseer is just a slave

That the Master respects so little that he is willing to give him a weapon

Today we call them

Rappers

Athletes

Politicians

Given Access, Money, and influence knowing all they will do,

Is give it right back,

Wouldn't dare bite the hand that feeds them,

But then there's never been any such thing,

As revolution with a corporate sponsor,

Never been any type of champion other than

The People's Champ,

But when corporations are people,

And people are measured in profit margins,

Are U a slave?

Think you Not a slave cuz you dred locked up,

Nigga you still locked up,

You might be woke,

But you still not up,

You sleep,

Listening to off beat rhythms tryna catch a beat,

Some semblance, some remembrance,

Of what you used to be,

But you,

Me

We

Don't even have a memory of Free,

Cause we are slaves,

Butterfly

she was born on the wrong side of the tracks
plus the wrong shade of black
from day one the odds were against her
and the deck was stacked
cuz mama had her own tracks and aside from that
before the bed was even cold poppa had his bags packed
like them rolling stones, all he left her was alone
just a couple chromosomes plus a head that was hard to comb
not that mom ever tried to
can't say she was lied to
cause it was plain as her clothes that she resented her arrival
essentially denied her the birthrights of any child
first words was street talk, cuz of her mama's life style
destined to be quite wild, her first high was in the womb
lullabies was mama's screams from the next room
at the hands of whatever man was over that night
after so many nights couldn't tell the fucks from the fights
the bruises from the love bites
love tap from a slap
worse than that, couldn't tell it wasn't supposed to be like that
cause momma hit the door be like "I'll be right back"
she wouldn't see that bitch for days then
that's why i find it amazin'
the situation she was raised in
so when i see her i bow my head and say this

(she's a butterfly up in the sky
gotta story to tell and i tell u why
she's searching…)

now as time moved on, her mind grew strong
had to determine for herself the path of right or wrong
walked the halls of her school tryna disguise her clothes
fuck a name brand she simply tryna hide them holes
cause BET and videos had defined her role

and when u young peer pressure be like mind control
and kids be oh so cold
they had to let her know
that she's as black as coal
and damn yo hair don't grow
none of them shots that they took was original
but they burnt just the same when they let them go
found the love of a man to try to heal her soul
i use the term love loosely
he just fucked her slow
she loved the way the penetration seemed to touch her soul
he loved the way her young lips never told him no
and just as quick as he came, it was time to go
saying keep that on the low while he out the door
she wasn't hurt by the fact that he aint want more
it was the closest thing to love that she had felt before
til that day she heard that voice moaning soft and low
vibrating through the speakers on her radio
speaking to her like a language from a kindred soul
putting words to all the pain that she had come to know
standing there in a zone like "how could they know"
then all at once in rush she just let it go
on the floor, chest heaving as the tears just flowed

(she's a butterfly up in the sky
gotta story to tell and i tell u why
she's searching…)

when she heard Denise sing it gave her strength to spread wings
brought to reality things that she had only dreamed
it seemed the words in the song they spoke to her
she had a new birth
closed her eyes and the song it spoke thru her
said be careful how you touch this wildflower might awake her
but it was too late
the chords and keys touched her nature
embraced her

made her safer than at home
standing at the open mic singing out redemption songs
for so long pain was the only feeling she had known
but when she opened up her mouth those feelings was gone
she felt the wrongs and sorrows in her soul melt away
swept away in melodies crafted by D. Hathaway
after days, nights, months and years feeling afflicted
the veil finally got lifted
she embraced being different
escaped the weight of self-hate
the sickness she had come to live with
she fell in love with the face in the mirror and her appearance
realized this was the package that the lord wrapped her gift in
and if them niggas aint like it
that's some shit they had to deal with
she was filled with the rage of a thousand hurricanes
something like the holy spirit
power raging thru her veins
she had made it through the storm
she survived with flying colors
once she got it through her head she aint need no one to love her
the only thing in this world she had to be was herself
you'll never find your direction in the eyes of someone else
she almost lost what was within looking for what was missing
and you can still hear her singing if you close ya eyes and listen

Dis Claim Her

If we did it,
If I submitted,
To this fleshly desire to devour you, ,,,,,If you,
gave in to,
Your curiosity,
Your cravings,
Make no mistake,
It would not, make me respect you any LESS,
But it also would not, make me love you any MORE,
This would be
A most divine love offering,
A physical expression, a reflection of my love and affection for all that
you are,
But please,
I ask that you do not confuse it with a promotion,
Don't get the notion,
That we are written in the stars,
Or that my touch is written in stone,
Kisses are not promisary notes,
We are not soulmates, no matter how deep the stroke,
I am not reading your mind,
I am reading the curvature of spine,
No matter how hard you cum,
No matter how many times,,,,,,,
This does not make you mine,
Orgasms do not legally bind,
Though my tongue may tie you,
I remind you,,,,,,,,
This is a moment in time,
Savour it,
Close yours EYES
TASTE the FEEL of my lips,
Against yours,
Breath us in,
SMELL the warmth of our skin,

LISTEN to me TASTE you,
as I WATCH the FEEL of your pleasure move you to SOUND,
Immerse the senses, untiil we're senseless,
As I broad brush stroke U,
Painting on your mental canvas for rememberence,
Of this savage tenderness, intimate ubiquitous,
Make your neck feel like a clitoris,
Just remember this,
is but a moment,
Defining neither you, I, nor this relationship,
This is a gift,
Treat it as such, Enjoy its touch, but not so much,
That you lose yourself,
If its between this feeling and your sanity,
I beg of you, choose yourself,
Do not fool yourself,
Into making fulltime investments for part time benefits,
Cum some to this moment, but do not succumb to it, , , ,,

Sundays We Sit In Silence

(inspired by Abi Bea ing)

on Sundays' we sit in silence
because we want to give words a rest
Monday thru Saturday we spend verbs, nouns, adjectives
with reckless abandon (word count is no object)
giving little to no consideration to our thoughts
before we deem them worthy of sound
worthy of repeating
worthy of subjecting others to them
if words have the ability to shape reality then our use of the English language is
nothing short of an abuse of power
a constant shower of odes to the obvious
exchanges of sweet nothings
or rubber check written by our mouths that our asses can't
or simply won't cash
said she loves me… no you don't
you love Obama
you love New York
you love cheesecake
you love Andre 3000,
you love that new Gucci Mane single
you love Hennessey
you love the block
hell you even love the way her ass fits in them jeans
but between politics, cheese cake, and ass
what the fuck does love even mean?
so on Sundays we sit in silence

on Sunday the pastor will ask you to steer clear of the mosque,
on Saturday the rabbi will rhetorically ask:
how can the church save you when the church itself is lost
on Friday I recall the imam warning me to steer clear of the wolves in Satan's
synagogue
but I have learned truth from them all so I KNOW them to be liars
bartering across pulpits with promises of hell fire or forgiveness

that they can't give you
6 hour sermons passing the basket 6 times to put new doors on a building that
stays locked 6 days out of the week
new bites with old knowledge that's new to them
old religion under a new name turning old tricks
policing your soul
attempting to arrest natural development
then hoping the charges stick
so when them squares come 'round we treat them like 5 O
we don't say shit
we just plead the fifth
and on Sundays we sit in silence

see the Sun hangs in the air
simultaneously warming and nurturing us in its radiance
while blinding and burning us in its power
an air that we can neither see nor touch yet we cannot live without
as we move on and in an earth that is more in sync with our bodies than we
providing not only food, clothing and shelter
but also the remedy to every malady that we inflict upon ourselves
in return we offer pollution and litter
under the title of civilization
tearing down a forest and replacing it with a nuclear reactor
silencing the symphonic harmony of nature
birds chirping… wind blowing softly thru trees
replacing it with the violent clamoring of the metropolis
doors slamming… sirens blaring
imagine the arrogance in tearing down an ecosystem
you neither understand nor can u reproduce
so you can build a university
so that you can teach what?
so that you can continue to stumble over, under and through words…
in an attempt to define, explain and give justification to that which predates you
by hundreds of thousands of centuries
so on Sundays we just sit…

Yo Mama

This poem is dedicated to
Yo Mama
See growing up on the North End of Detroit things sometimes got hard
We didn't have a lot of money
We didn't have nice clothes or a car
Hell sometimes we didn't even have electricity
But we always had YO MAMA
See back before there was a PS2 or 3
Back when Wii was just something you said when ya uncle ray pushed you on
the swings
Before we could even afford an Atari
We knew YO MAMA was all the entertainment we would ever need
On the front porch where we used to exchange caps
but not the type of caps that would push ya wig back
YO MAMA was always in attendance
Making us all feel like Lil Eddie Murphy's or Chris Thomas from BET
"Man yo' Mama so fat that if she jumped in the air she would get stuck"
"Shoot, yo Mama so ugly that when she was born the Dr. slapped her daddy."
"Hey Maaan, let's just get off Mama's. Shoot I just got offa yours."
YO MAMA would watch over us on long summer days
keeping us out of the streets and off of the news
There with me as moves took me to 10 different schools in 12 years
When I was the new kid on the playground
and all the cool kids were cracking on me cause I talked funny
or dressed different or I was in the free lunch line
and all the pretty girls were staring
and the only thing I could think to say was...
"YA MAMA"
and the whole playground erupted in laughter instantly
see, YO MAMA was internationally known
world recognized and hood certified
in every ghetto, barrio, project, or block
Way before 50, Biggie, or even Tupac
EVERYBODY knew YO MAMA
(no really dog EVERYBODY knew YO MAMA)

And as time moved forward
and playgrounds gave way to boardrooms, and trap houses
air force ones gave way to Stacey Adams, work boots
and bigger air force ones
huffys and ten speed gave way to 24 inch spinning rims
car notes and maybe, just maybe insurance
Best friends, play cousins, and blood brothers and sisters who grew up together
grew apart
traveling different roads
wearing different hats
father
wife
doctor
pastor
the defendant
manager
sergeant
victim
suspect…
But I still see it all through the eyes of a child
I still see you
before the locs, before the glasses, yeah about fifty pounds lighter
I still see 100 Marston, Bright Meyer Elementary, and Mr. Fofo's Deli
Sometimes I, even still, ghost ride the shopping carts through the parking lot at
King Cole
And that rare occasion when you call me
that once every blue moon
and you ask what's up
I will still respond
"YO MAMA"

Little boy in line at Family Dollar Haiku

I see him there sad
small boy already broken
looks like my sons age

His mom just as lost,
Her words cut him like daggers,
Passing pains to him,

Wish I could take him,
Give him a hug from a man,
Look him in his eyes,

Where is his Father,
The worst kind of betrayal,
He knows his burden,

Pray that he makes it,
As Mom pays at the counter,
"Bring your dumb ass on!"

(I saw this specific scene when I was at the Family Dollar on Gratiot next to the Better Made Chip Factory, but I have seen it a million times. Momma already angry for God knows what. I'm no one to judge; maybe it's a valid reason maybe it's not. But I find it hard to imagine the child can be responsible to the degree he is paying for it. I always just wonder where the Dad is. Like, you know this woman is not fun to be around because you not around her, but you leave your son to deal with her. Alone. No Greater Betrayal.)

The Plan of Allah

the irony was not lost on me…
we had come to save him
this boy
this young man, who now hung from the rafters in the basement like a martyr
arms tied to the rafters
body dangling back and forth like a broken tree limb
sweat trickling down his forehead
mixing with his tears
resting momentarily on his chin
and then falling to the ground
as his body shivered
every few moments

we, his captors in a semi-circle around
all brown, like he
and we
we had come to save him
the banners on our 20 or so businesses around the city said as much
UNITED NATION OF ISLAM
DOING RIGHT FOR THE RIGHT REASON
BUILDING A NATION

"well you tell me!
what kind of nation can't protect its women and its children!"
these were the words on the lips of every captain and lieutenant in Kansas after
that brick had been lofted from the corner of 13th and Quindaro
striking the window on our school bus
raining shards of glass down on the faces and hair of the sisters and babies
on their way to MGT class
before the last bits of glass had been picked from the sisters' hair
we, the mighty FOI, had hit the streets like an occupational army
doors kicked in
cars pulled over
insurgents apprehended

pulled from homes and interrogated using the latest in homegrown techniques
ironic that we had escaped places like
Detroit, Newark, Chicago, Long Beach, Brooklyn
to come here to Kansas in the name of saving our people
the very same people we now engaged in outright warfare with

"when you know the plan of Allah, you will go places that you don't want to go, do
things you don't want to do, and talk to people you don't want to talk to."
less than 24 hours later we had our man
and the time for talking had come and gone
our instructions were clear
we needed that hand
the one that had thrown that brick
all too often in the affairs of nations and God
liberation can turn into occupation
education can turn into assimilation
five broken fingers can turn into a separated shoulder
five cracked ribs
a young black boy who will never ever walk again

history teaches us that none make greater tyrants than the victims of tyranny
politicians speak of passing on budget deficits to our grandchildren
but what of the true debt incurred in warfare
for somewhere in Palestine a future suicide bomber returns home to find
a pile of rubble in the space where his mother once nursed his baby sister
in central Africa two teenagers who could pass for brothers
biologically and genetically
exchange gunfire
playing the latest roles in a cyclical genocide that predates them by 100 years

and in Kansas City
one young man will pay for the foolishness and immaturity of youth
with his ability to walk
while another, in search of nationhood and salvation, finds himself lost
a million miles from humanity

(This is a persona piece based on my experience inside of the United Nation of Islam. The following is an excerpt from my book The Perks of Cult Life or why I had to slap brother Ronnie 7 times. They both deal with what may be considered extreme actions but the principle is the same; when we ignore what we know to be right in order to fit into a social order we invariably lose.)

When You Know the Plan of Allah

The following is an excerpt from "The Perks of Cult Life or why I had to slap brother Ronnie 7 times.

"When you know the plan of Allah you will, go places you don't want to go, do things you don't want to do, and talk to people you don't want to talk to."

This lesson stuck with me as I matriculated through the United Nation of Islam. As the Minister of the Detroit Temple I quoted this often to members who had occasionally met their assignment with a bit of reluctance. It accurately summed up the idea that once you had written your savior's letter declaring allegiance to Royall, Allah in Person, you essentially gave up free will and agreed to do whatever was needed to be in harmony with Royall's will. The problem often was that by the time his will made it through the many links and kinks in the chain of command, it had been manipulated by the politics that existed in the UNOI.

My most challenging experience with this lesson came when I arrived at the bakery for duty in the Fall of 2008. It was early in the week so there were only two fundraiser teams going out. The first was Brother Minister Thomas: a humble brother originally from Atlanta, Georgia. The second was Brother Ronnie, from Kansas City. Both brothers had been followers of the Honorable Elijah Muhammad during the 60s and 70s and now in the UNOI had been sent to Detroit to help us move things forward. Both brothers had been quite a bit of help, Ronnie in particular. While Thomas had quite a bit of knowledge and a very friendly spirit, his lack of understanding of UNOI politics and watching his wife die under UNOI care had left him somewhat docile and hesitant. Ronnie was a brother after my own heart. In Heaven (UNOI headquarters in Kansas City, KS)

31

he was one of the first brothers to take me under his wing. Though he had long ago turned his life over to Allah, if you spent ten minutes in his presence you could tell he was a street wise, tough guy. In Ronnie I finally had someone willing to hurt a few feelings and say what needed to be said in order to end the lackadaisical attitudes that had made Detroit the laughing stock of the UNOI.

As the members began to trickle in to begin their duties, my phone rang.
"As Salaam Alaikum"
"Wa Laikum Salaam"
It was Sister Julie.
"Sister Sandy wants to come in and help in the bakery. Is that okay?"
I rolled my eyes.
"Absolutely, the more the merrier!"
"Okay, I will call and tell her."
We gave the greetings and got off of the phone.

Sister Sandy had been processing for the last three months. Already she was one of the more diligent and serious participants in the Temple. She regularly called to find out what was needed duty wise, gave more charity than most of the members, actively participated in class and brought visitors.

My trepidation stemmed from the off and on again affair that she and I had carried on for the past three years. Though this type of behavior was nothing new for me, I had broken one of the cardinal rules for brothers that did venture outside the Nation to sow their wild oats. I had told her who I was and what I was about, even worse I began to teach her. Once she began to look for more than the intense physical trysts that existed between us, she found her way to class, and started orientation. When she cut of her long flowing locs per UNOI policy, I knew I was in trouble.

Nevertheless, once she began processing I warned her not to expect anything more from me and effectively ended our physical interactions. I let her know that what we had done was a matter of my personal indiscretion and nothing more. She said she understood and promptly began to apply herself to the nation like a woman possessed. As glad as I was to see her there, I was equally worried that she was there for all the wrong reasons.

Sandy arrived around 10am and I asked her to get the teams' baked goods together. As usual she checked with the brothers to see what they needed, and the brothers were promptly out on their way. I stood in front of the bakery labeling cookies, when Sandy walked in from the back. She stood there silently for a moment so I turned and asked her, "What's up?"

"I don't think I like Brother Ronnie very much."

"Aw, Brother Ronnie's just a lil misunderstood, he's good people."

"I don't think I misunderstand him. I just don't want to be around him anymore"

"What do you mean? What happened?"

"He just kissed my hand."

I paused not sure if I heard her correctly. She repeated it. I cursed. She said that after helping to put together his order Ronnie had stopped to thank her and in doing so, grabbed her hand and kissed it. I sighed and weighed my options. The justice system in the UNOI, much like that of the world, often times worked differently depending who was in the know about a particular crime. In this case, a married brother kissed the hand of a sister that was processing, and here the sister was telling me about it. I would just as soon tell her to forget about it, it won't happen again, but then all I needed was for the Sister's military to think I was trying to hide or protect brothers who sexually harassed sisters. Not with my reputation.

"Okay, well you need to call Sister Julie."

She hesitated, "I don't want to get him trouble"

"Well, at this point you have already told me, and I can't address it without directing you to the proper channels so… "

She said she understood and that she would call as soon as she got home. I walked her to the car and called Kaaba, the National Lt.

"As Salaam, what's up Pros?"

I sighed.

"Aw shit. What happened?"

I explained the scenario to him. He replied that this didn't bode well for Ronnie, who apparently already had a reputation. These days they were putting people out of the nation for less. I stressed how vital Ronnie had been to our success and how losing him would set us back greatly. Kaaba said he would do what he could to get ahead of the curve on this one. I thanked him and told him I would be waiting on his call.

The rest of the day passed pretty much normally. The beat down look on Ronnie's face when he came in let me know that he had already received the first wave of conference calls that typically unfolded, courtesy of Kaaba and the other National Officials anytime there was any major scenario. We didn't speak much other than him turning in the funds for the day and heading home. I closed the bakery at 9pm and headed home.

The scenario was just about out of my head, when I walked through the door to the customary calls of "Daddddy!!!" from my three sons. My wife appeared at the top of the stairs with the house phone.
"Kaaba asked you to call him."
I took the phone and stepped back out onto the porch to dial Kaaba's number.
"Okay, here is the deal"
"Yessir"
"In order for Ronnie to stay he is going to need to get popped in the mouth seven times."
Seven was the God number, and corporal punishment was not a new idea in the Nation. I pulled my coat back on and called Kaaba from my cell as he tried to explain the proper way to smack Brother Ronnie.
"Hard enough to make his mouth bleed, but not hard enough to swell his lip. Use the back of the hand, make sure you can feel his teeth through his lips with your knuckle. Hard enough to where he can't talk, but not so hard that he can't go to duty tomorrow."
If I didn't know what we were talking about, I would have thought he was joking. I parked in front of Ronnie's home, went to the door and asked him to step outside for a minute. I walked to the back of the house and waited on him.
When Ronnie finally arrived I called Kaaba on three way, and he then connected Bro Captain Rodney of Kansas. We all exchanged the greeting and Bro Kaaba began:
"Alright, we all spoke earlier, I hope you understand the severity of what you did today."
Brother Ronnie spoke in his characteristic Midwestern twang, "Yessir. I definitely understand and this will not happen again. I can guarantee you that much."
Rodney spoke, "The problem is Ronnie, we had this conversation before and you said the same thing, so something more is going to be needed to stress the point."

34

Kaaba picked up the conversation," Ronnie you can either, leave right now, pack your things and get out of the Nation's home, or Bro Minister is going to have to smack you in the mouth seven times."

Ronnie didn't hesitate, "Oh, yes, sir. I don't want to leave so I will have to take the smacks."

"You're sure?"

"I mean, I don't want to get slapped but if that's only way I can stay..."

"Alright, Brother Prostell, you there?"

"Yessir"

"You can go ahead and get started. Be sure to hold the phone up so that we can hear."

I walked over to Brother Ronnie. Holding the phone up with my left hand, I brought my right hand back, and delivered the first slap to Ronnie's mouth. POP! I could feel his rough skin and moustache recoil against the back of my hand. POP! POP! POP! He seemed to flinch uniquely with every hit. POP! POP! POP!

"That's it" I said.

"You started? I didn't hear anything?"

Now I was getting irritated. "Do I need to do it again?"

"Ronnie, he hit you?"

"Yeffr" Ronnie responded sucking his lip.

"Is your lip bleeding?"

"Yeffr"

"Maaaaan, are you lying Ronnie?"

"No sir, I am not. That hurt."

"Damn Prostell, you slapped him all seven times that quick?"

"Yessir"

"You must have been on the speed slapping team in college or something."

I was speechless.

Ronnie spoke up again," He definitely hit me and it definitely hurt."

"Yeah right."

"Look, I did it, if you need me to do it again slower, just say that... "

"Alright, alright, alright, alright, Ronnie you need to go ahead and get ready for tomorrow and I will call you and let you know what the verdict is. Prostell, we will call you right back."

"Yessir" we both responded.

As we walked back toward the front of the house Brother Ronnie apologized repeatedly for putting me in this situation. I assured him that I had been in my share of the same type of scenario, but that we needed to put this situation behind us and do what we came to Detroit to do. The irony of a man who was like an uncle to me apologizing for me having slapped him, for kissing the hand of a sister that I had carried on a three year affair with was not lost on me. I repeated to myself as I got in the car, "When you know the plan of Allah... "

Post log
As I drove away from the house I dialed Kaaba. He answered in a surprisingly pleasant tone that belied the circumstances we had just spoken under. "Yes"
"Please tell me you have good news."
He laughed, "Maaan, Ronnie not in trouble." I could hear Captain Rodney laughing in the background.
"But once they find out we made this punishment up, we might be."

Acknowledgments

Let me start by saying I *WILL* miss someone.
I just will.
Someone vitally important to the success of not only this project but to me as an artist. So can we just get that out of the way?
I'm Sorry.
There are far too many people that play a vital role in these poetic and artistic communities to name and in so many ways I am a product of these artistic communities so if you bought a book, CD, painting, ticket, palm reading, interpretive lap dance, product, like a fan page, status, shared a link, booked a show, gave discount to, let one crash on your couch the from every artist anywhere on this planet I Thank You!
Not only have you supported their individual efforts but you have helped to maintain an ever shrinking, but much needed Market Place of Truth and Ideas.

More specifically
Detroit:
Lashuan Phoenix Moore, thank you for making this real to me, for the safe space, and the open door.
Daune Smith and Diallo Smith thank you both for believing in my art before I was even sure what it was. Thank you both for the continued light you shine unto the world.
D Blair for setting the bar
Nandi, Omari King Wise, Ray, Fluent, T. Miller, Jamaal Versus May, Honeycomb, Mic Write, Mic Phelps, Dimonique Boyd, Cassie Poe, Whitney Syphax Walker, Beautiful Thought, Chico, Caesar, Shawn Moore-Bey, Soltreu, Untitled, Kevlar, Ju Hall, Adaora, BBMC, Deonte Osayande, Blk Smith, Knowledge, Mental, G Smoove, Freeway, Kjai Sanders, Fara Moan, Numi, Clarity, Berhenda Williams, Thomas Williams, Jar, Alexis Draper, Mike Will, Ben Jones, Lucky Lefty, Kash Marlinowski, J Della, Gaius, Kasey Bean, Captain Dave , ok, look Im not doing this I'd be here all night, They got me paying by the page in here yall, , , Detroit Stand UP!!!

Orlando:
Hopewell you way more than poetry Fam so sorry I can't even mention you in this space.
Shawn Welcome, thank you for being a beacon of light and

37

revolutionary in such positive ways.
Blu Bailey for always being of service
Kyla Lacey something smart
Jason Alexander for understanding the hustle.
Bailey B. being new
Autumn Blaze 333
. Moses West, Ambrose Cavender, Curtis Meyer, Tim Rumsey,
Mckinnon, Miss Write, V.A. Johnty, Nas, Danni Cassette, Mosaic, Rob
Bradley, Wally B, MyVerse, Viviana and Fam, Envy Hair Designs, Jajose,
VeTo, Kindred, Charisse Middleton, Tiffany Sanford, Laquita Langley,
Bird Sanders, Melanie, Kierah, Neon

Denver:
Lady Speech for being as deep and plentiful as the Universe itself
Slam Nuba, thanks for raising the bar
Mercury Café being a safe place for weirdoes like me
Lenny the right words at the right time only always.
Aset Uno So you mean to teeeell me,,,
Lucifury, Jovan, Bianca Mikhan, Dominique, Piper, Mary McDonough,
Jamrock Gypsy, Shy, Oxygen, Franklin, Noah, Peter Reed, Dominique
Ashley,
To each and every person that supported this project or my journey in
any way
I Thank You.

* 9 7 8 0 6 1 5 8 4 0 8 7 1 *